Strange Creatures of the Sea
COLORING BOOK

Llyn Hunter

Dover Publications, Inc.
New York

Introduction

Since the dawn of time, the sea has been a source of mystery and fear. All cultures and peoples living near the ocean have had their legends of its monsters or serpents. In centuries past, disappearances of sailing vessels were often blamed on such monsters, and strange carcasses that would wash ashore or be brought up from deep waters seemed to confirm these beliefs.

Within the pages of this book you will discover animals from the ocean's depths that may have been the source of old sea-serpent tales, bizarre fish with alien features that seem more like space creatures than dwellers on planet Earth, and fearful beings that threaten the lives of divers who dare enter their realm.

Today, with vehicles that can take us ever deeper below the waves, we are constantly learning more about these mysteries. And recent discoveries indicate that there are many more strange creatures of the sea waiting to be found.

Alphabetical List of Common Names

Alphabetical List of Scientific Names

Copyright © 1991 by Dover Publications, Inc.

All rights reserved under Pan American and International Copyright Conventions.

Published in Canada by General Publishing Company, Ltd., 30 Lesmill Road, Don Mills, Toronto, Ontario.

Published in the United Kingdom by Constable and Company, Ltd., 3 The Lanchesters, 162–164 Fulham Palace Road, London W6 9ER.

Strange Creatures of the Sea Coloring Book is a new work, first published by Dover Publications, Inc., in 1991.

DOVER *Pictorial Archive* SERIES

This book belongs to the Dover Pictorial Archive Series. You may use the designs and illustrations for graphics and crafts applications, free and without special permission, provided that you include no more than four in the same publication or project. (For permission for additional use, please write to Dover Publications, Inc., 31 East 2nd Street, Mineola, N.Y. 11501.)

However, republication or reproduction of any illustration by any other graphic service whether it be in a book or in any other design resource is strictly prohibited.

International Standard Book Number: 0-486-26836-5

Manufactured in the United States of America
Dover Publications, Inc., 31 East 2nd Street, Mineola, N.Y. 11501

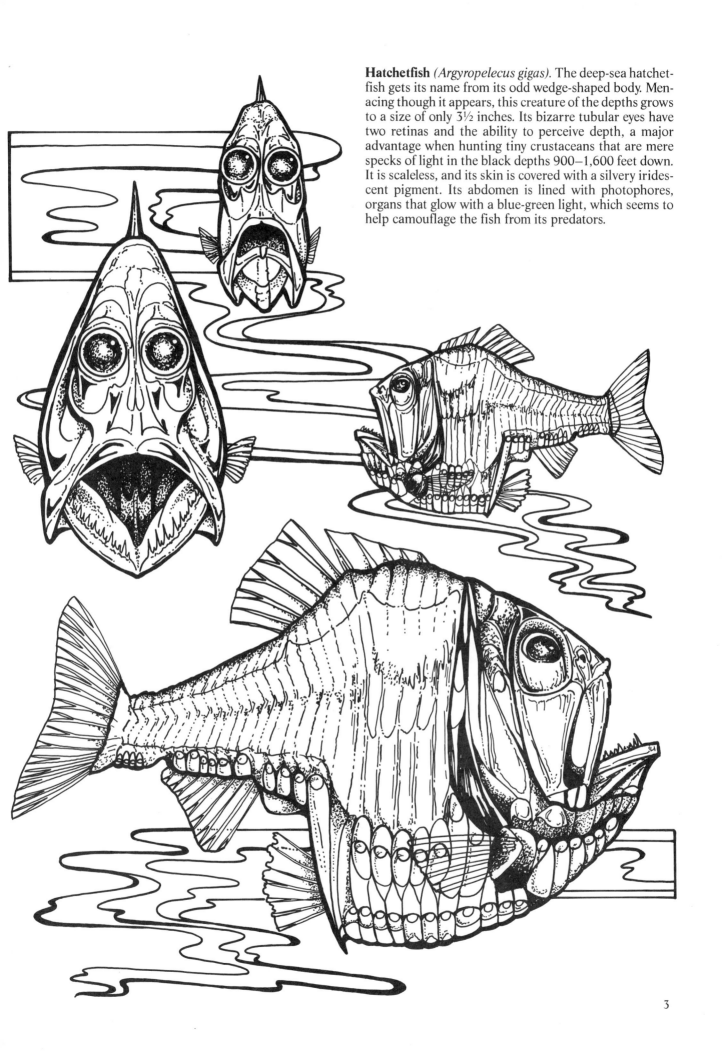

Hatchetfish *(Argyropelecus gigas).* The deep-sea hatchetfish gets its name from its odd wedge-shaped body. Menacing though it appears, this creature of the depths grows to a size of only 3½ inches. Its bizarre tubular eyes have two retinas and the ability to perceive depth, a major advantage when hunting tiny crustaceans that are mere specks of light in the black depths 900–1,600 feet down. It is scaleless, and its skin is covered with a silvery iridescent pigment. Its abdomen is lined with photophores, organs that glow with a blue-green light, which seems to help camouflage the fish from its predators.

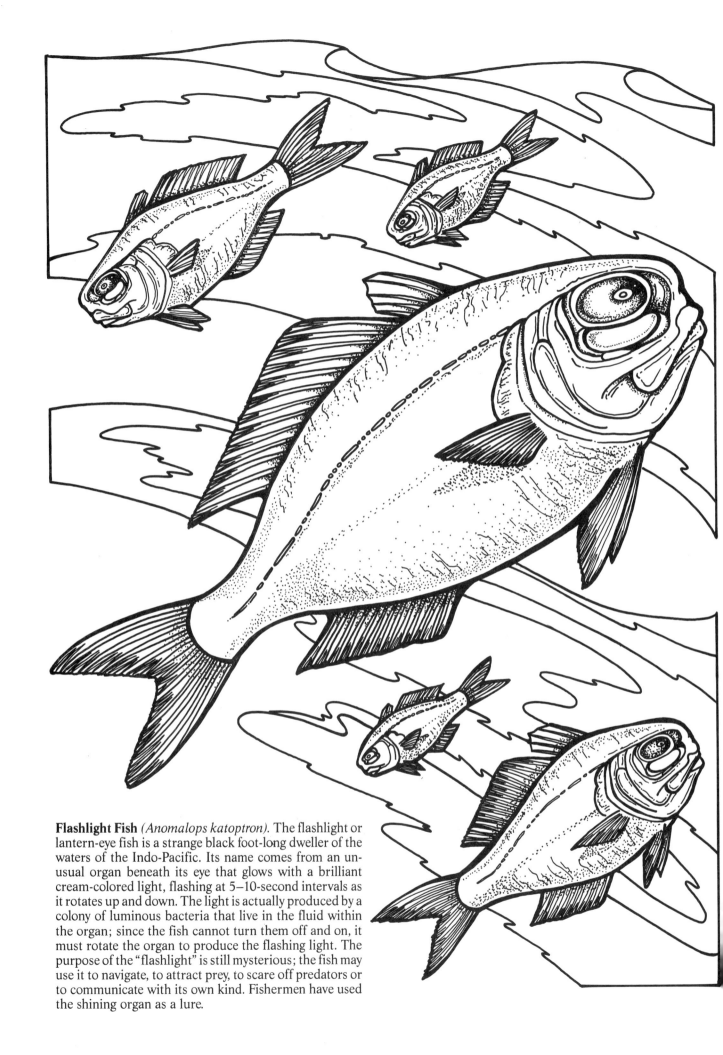

Flashlight Fish *(Anomalops katoptron).* The flashlight or lantern-eye fish is a strange black foot-long dweller of the waters of the Indo-Pacific. Its name comes from an unusual organ beneath its eye that glows with a brilliant cream-colored light, flashing at 5–10-second intervals as it rotates up and down. The light is actually produced by a colony of luminous bacteria that live in the fluid within the organ; since the fish cannot turn them off and on, it must rotate the organ to produce the flashing light. The purpose of the "flashlight" is still mysterious; the fish may use it to navigate, to attract prey, to scare off predators or to communicate with its own kind. Fishermen have used the shining organ as a lure.

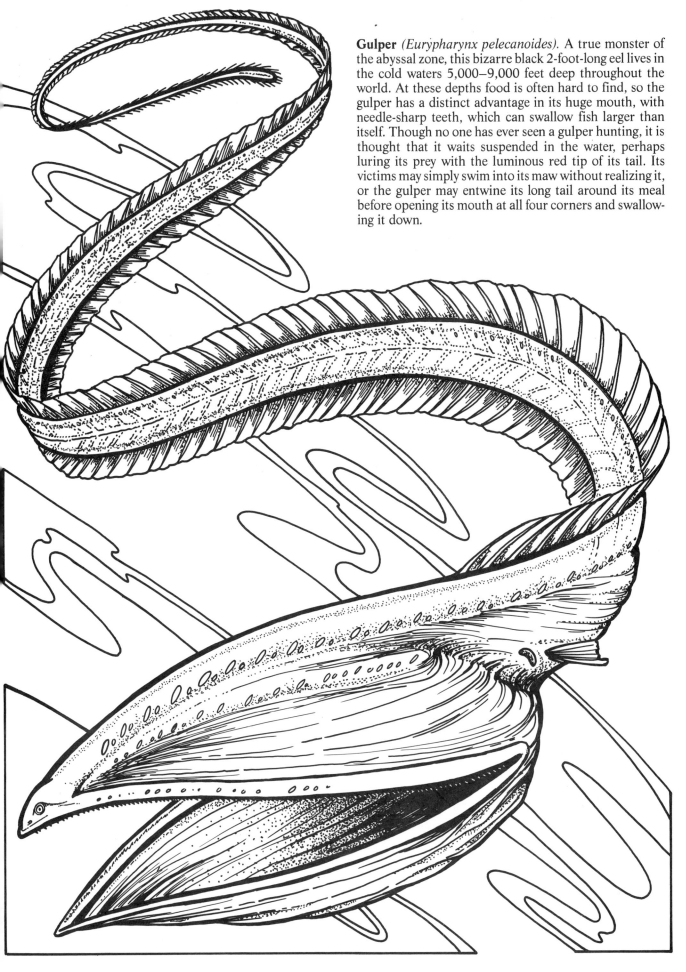

Gulper *(Eurypharynx pelecanoides)*. A true monster of the abyssal zone, this bizarre black 2-foot-long eel lives in the cold waters 5,000–9,000 feet deep throughout the world. At these depths food is often hard to find, so the gulper has a distinct advantage in its huge mouth, with needle-sharp teeth, which can swallow fish larger than itself. Though no one has ever seen a gulper hunting, it is thought that it waits suspended in the water, perhaps luring its prey with the luminous red tip of its tail. Its victims may simply swim into its maw without realizing it, or the gulper may entwine its long tail around its meal before opening its mouth at all four corners and swallowing it down.

Deep-Sea Anglers (top to bottom: *Melanocetus cirrifer,*
Lasiognathus saccostoma, Borophryne apogon, Lino-
phryne macrodon). Living at depths of 3,000–12,000
feet, these brown or black 2½–4-inch anglers are truly
deep-sea fishermen. In each species, part of the dorsal fin
has moved to the front of the head and developed muscles
and appendages, enabling the fish to use it like a rod and
lure to attract prey. In most species the rod glows with a
blue-green light produced by bacteria in its cells. *Bor-*
ophryne apogon, like some other anglers, is also odd in its
reproductive habits. The male will attach himself with his
mouth to the much larger female early in life; his own
body will then slowly degenerate as he becomes a parasite
on the female, feeding off her bloodstream.

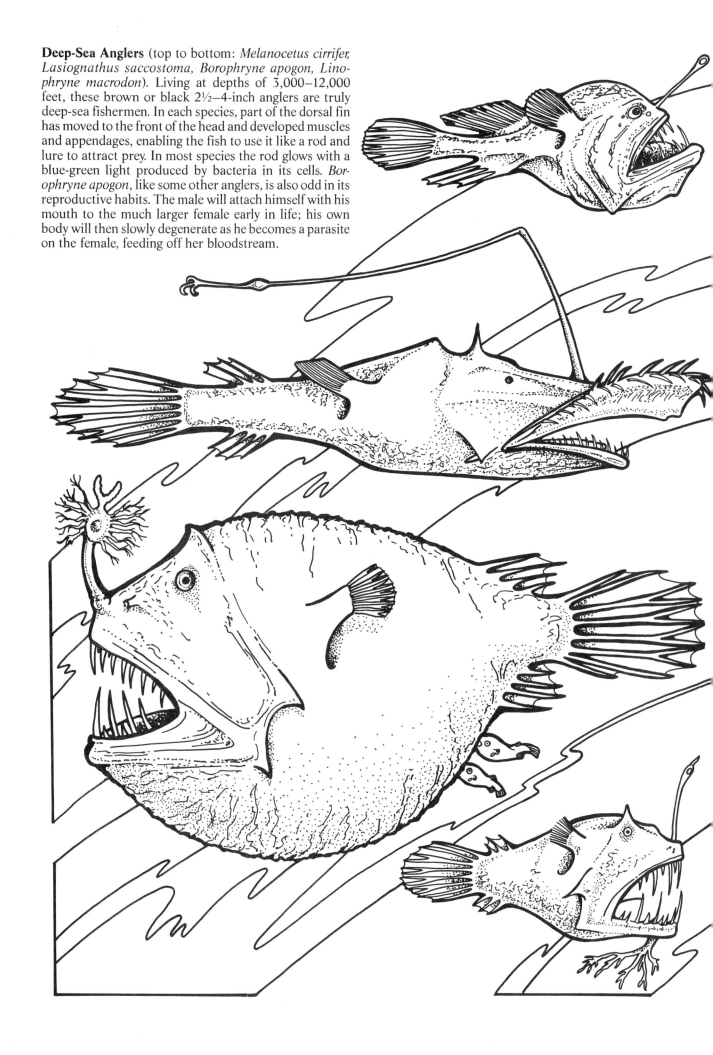

Viperfish *(Chauliodus sloani).* The viperfish belongs to a family of vicious-looking deep-sea dwellers that range in size from a few inches to almost a foot, like this one. These small but effective predators live at depths of 2,000–5,000 feet during the day and migrate vertically to about 500 feet at night, feeding on shrimp, small crustaceans and fish. The viperfish ranges in color from silver to black; the photophores that cover the roof of its mouth and form a double row along the sides glow blue-green.

Brotulids *(Acanthonus armatus, Typhlonus nasus).* The brotulids are among the most diverse and widespread of the deep-sea fishes, numbering about 150 species. Most brotulids have a big head that tapers to a long pointed tail, and a fin that continues unbroken around the tail. They tend to get smaller the deeper they live. The three-foot *Acanthonus armatus* (top) is creamy brown and semi-transparent; it lives in the 8,000-foot depths off the African coast. *Typhlonus nasus,* at 6 inches, is much smaller, similarly semitransparent and completely blind; it can be found as deep as 16,300 feet in the Celebes Sea.

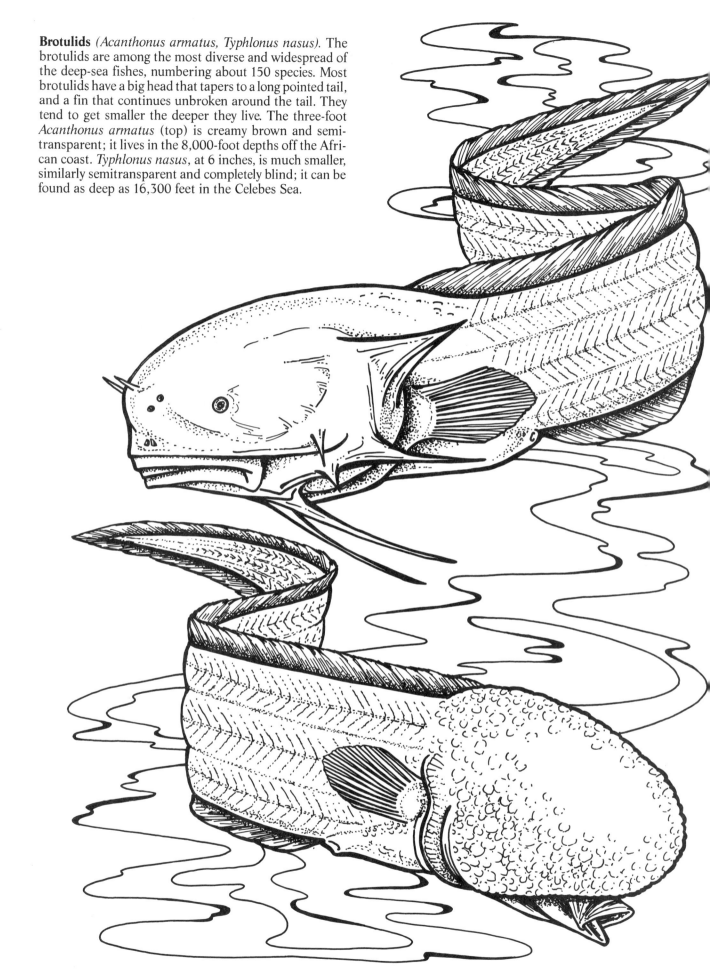

Coelacanth *(Latimeria chalumnae)*. The coelacanth, which may have existed as far back as 400 million years ago, was long thought to have been extinct for close to 60 million years. Then in 1938 one of these "living fossils" was caught in a trawl off the coast of South Africa. The coelacanth is difficult to find because it lives on the bottom 300–600 feet down, near the Comoro Islands. It is steel-blue with light-cream patches. It may weigh almost 200 pounds and measure 6 feet in length. Scientists believe that it was from lobe-finned fishes like the coelacanth that the first land-dwelling animals evolved.

9

Oarfish *(Regalecus glesne)*. The oarfish has surely been the inspiration for many sea-serpent stories. Normally found in deep waters, it will occasionally come near the surface, where it can be seen swimming in an undulating, serpentine fashion. The larger individuals, 20–30 feet long, could easily be taken for reptilian monsters. But this apparent monster is actually a gentle giant, eating only crustaceans and small fish. Its spectacular fins are bright red and its body is translucent blue-gray with dark stripes.

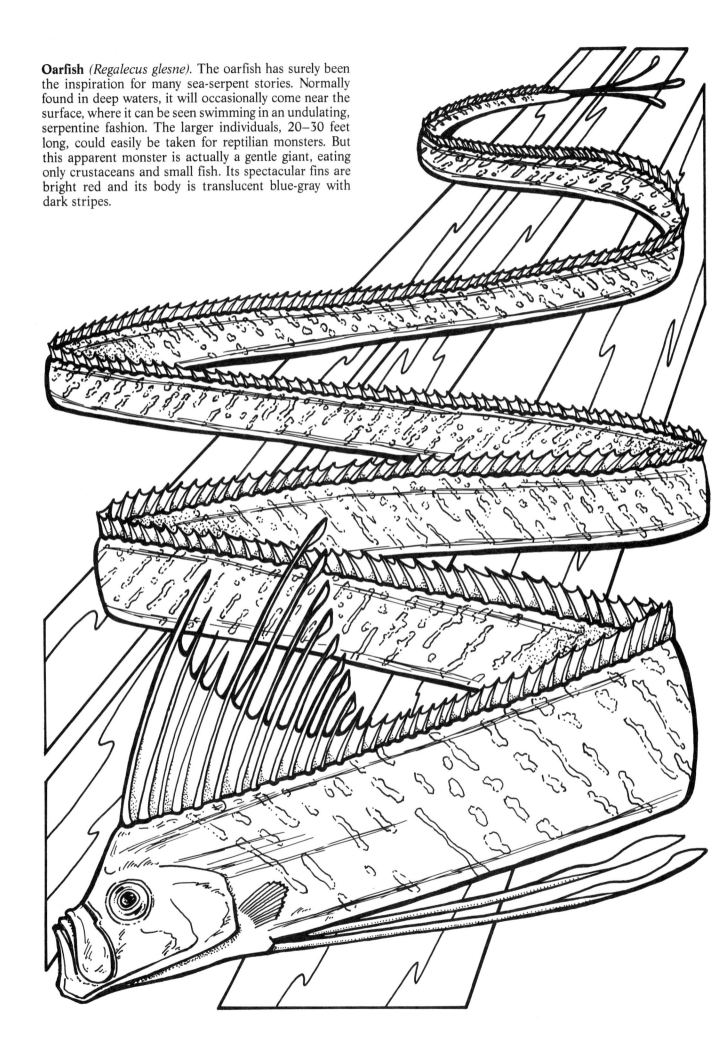

Snake Mackerel *(Gempylus serpens).* The deep-sea snake mackerel—not a true mackerel—is a serpentlike fish that lives at depths of around 2,000 feet. Its great stiletto teeth and protruding lower jaw give it a menacing appearance similar to another predator, the barracuda. The snake mackerel ranges in color from light ruddy gray to black, and in size from 2½ to 5 feet. It is widespread throughout the Atlantic, primarily in temperate and tropical waters. Its flesh is considered a delicacy in Spain.

Giant Squid *(Architeuthis princeps)*. The brick-red giant squid—probably the terrifying "kraken" of Swedish legend—has been known to grow to 57 feet and may weigh over 4 tons. Its eye is the size of a beach ball. It normally lives in the deep ocean and is rarely seen on the surface; when provoked, however, it has the strength to pull a good-sized dinghy beneath the waves. It has eight regular tentacles; two longer tentacles with special suction cups and retractable claws are used for capturing prey. Scars from these claws have often been found on sperm whales, consequences of deep-sea battles.

Giant Pacific Octopus *(Octopus dofleini).* Often considered one of the ugliest of the sea's creatures, the octopus has unjustly acquired a bad reputation. For years it was claimed that the giant octopus would grab divers and take them to a watery grave. The truth is that even this giant, which may weigh over 125 pounds and whose tentacle spread may occasionally reach 30 feet, is very shy and would rather flee in a cloud of black ink than attack. One explanation for supposed attacks is that the animal will sometimes "explore" a diver out of curiosity. If the diver tries to pull its tentacles off, it will grip tighter as a natural response; if ignored, it will satisfy its curiosity and simply swim away.

13

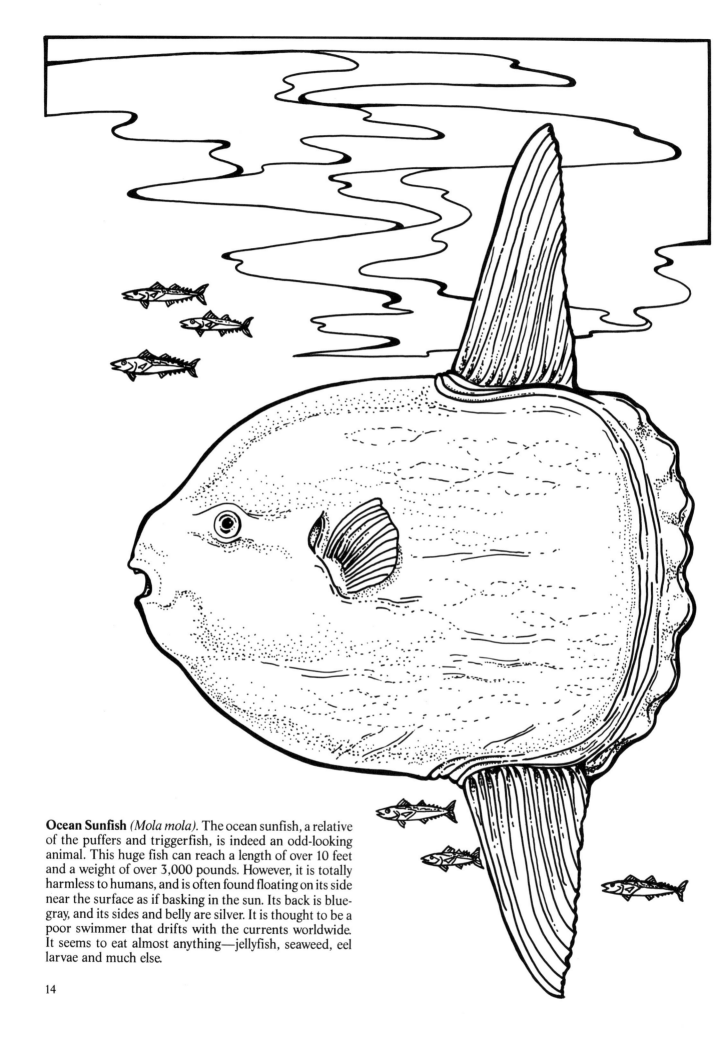

Ocean Sunfish *(Mola mola).* The ocean sunfish, a relative of the puffers and triggerfish, is indeed an odd-looking animal. This huge fish can reach a length of over 10 feet and a weight of over 3,000 pounds. However, it is totally harmless to humans, and is often found floating on its side near the surface as if basking in the sun. Its back is blue-gray, and its sides and belly are silver. It is thought to be a poor swimmer that drifts with the currents worldwide. It seems to eat almost anything—jellyfish, seaweed, eel larvae and much else.

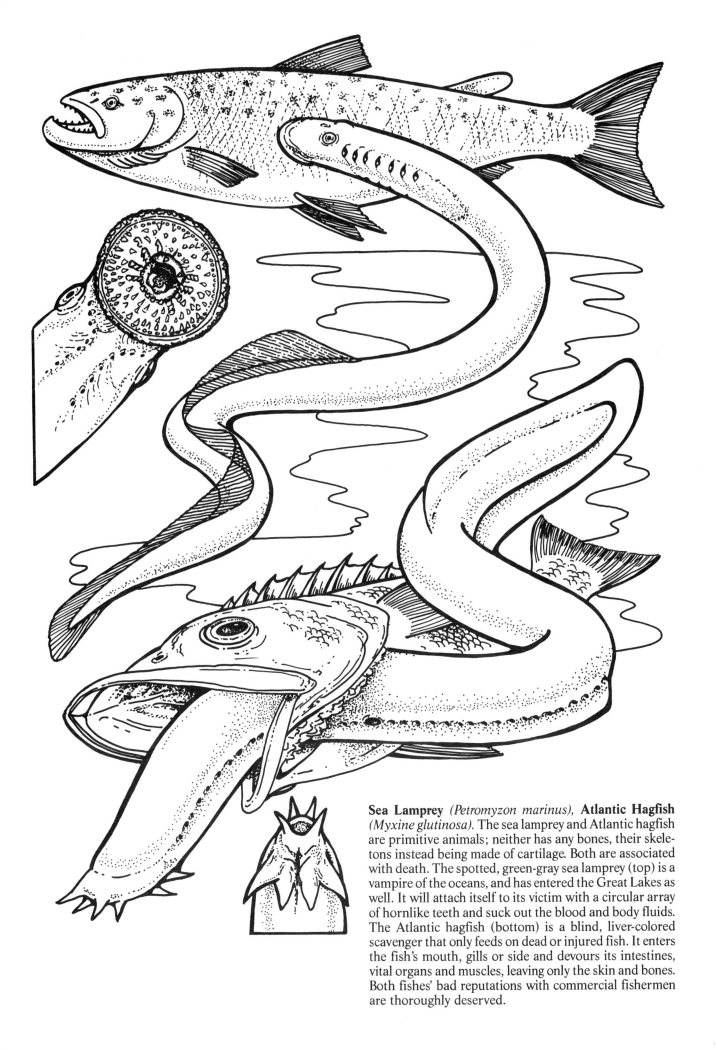

Sea Lamprey *(Petromyzon marinus)*, **Atlantic Hagfish**
(Myxine glutinosa). The sea lamprey and Atlantic hagfish
are primitive animals; neither has any bones, their skeletons instead being made of cartilage. Both are associated
with death. The spotted, green-gray sea lamprey (top) is a
vampire of the oceans, and has entered the Great Lakes as
well. It will attach itself to its victim with a circular array
of hornlike teeth and suck out the blood and body fluids.
The Atlantic hagfish (bottom) is a blind, liver-colored
scavenger that only feeds on dead or injured fish. It enters
the fish's mouth, gills or side and devours its intestines,
vital organs and muscles, leaving only the skin and bones.
Both fishes' bad reputations with commercial fishermen
are thoroughly deserved.

California Scorpionfish *(Scorpaena guttata),* **Stonefish** *(Synanceja verrucosa).* These two creatures come from the most venomous family of fishes. The hollow spines of their dorsal fins, if stepped on, will inject a poison that can cause severe injury and often death. Both are about 1–1½ feet long and are mottled in shades of red, brown and black. They live among the rocks well camouflaged, lying in wait for fish to prey upon. The California scorpionfish (top) is found along the Pacific coast; even with its venomous spines, it is considered a good sport fish. The stonefish (bottom) of the Indo-Pacific region is renowned as one of the most dangerous of its clan. Since it lives in shallow water, it has been the cause of many fatal accidents.

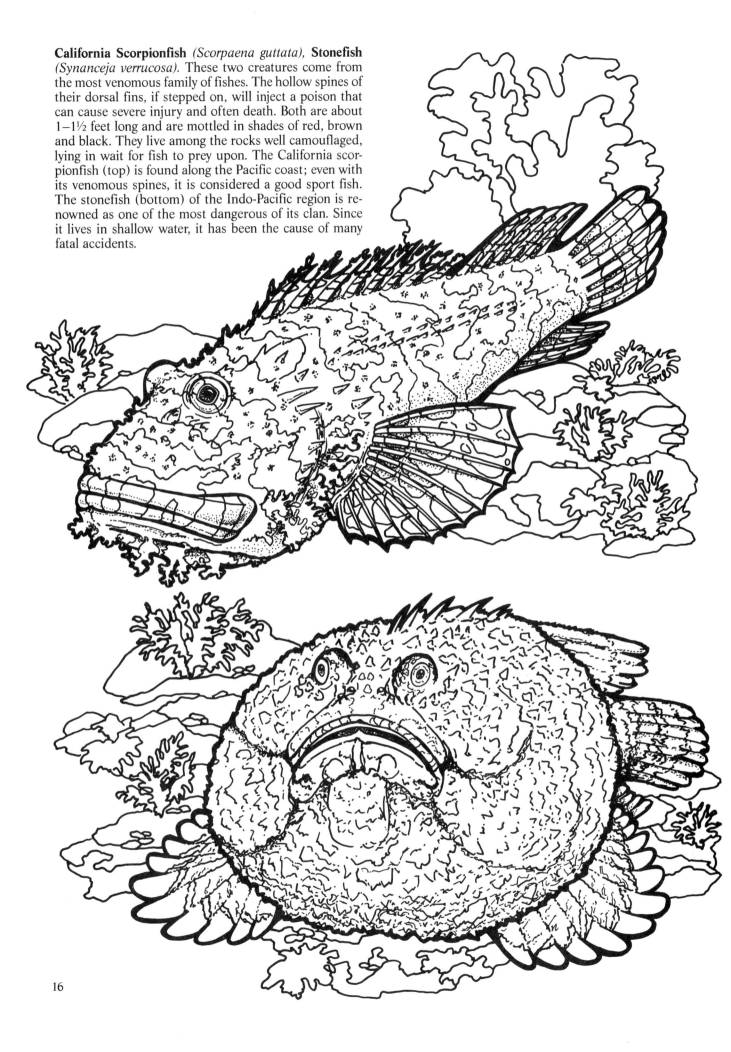

16

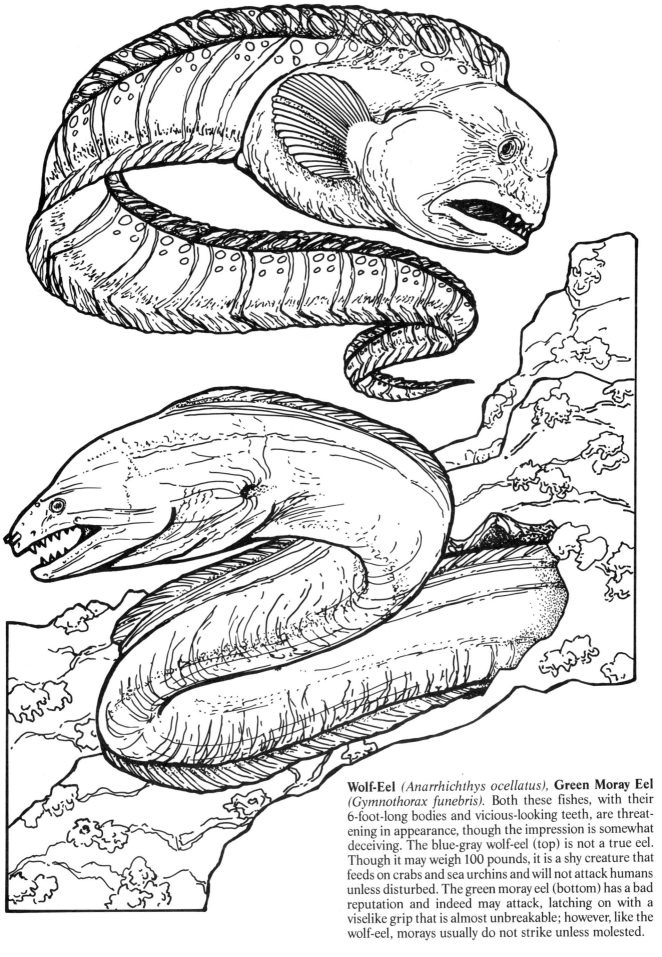

Wolf-Eel (*Anarrhichthys ocellatus*), **Green Moray Eel** (*Gymnothorax funebris*). Both these fishes, with their 6-foot-long bodies and vicious-looking teeth, are threatening in appearance, though the impression is somewhat deceiving. The blue-gray wolf-eel (top) is not a true eel. Though it may weigh 100 pounds, it is a shy creature that feeds on crabs and sea urchins and will not attack humans unless disturbed. The green moray eel (bottom) has a bad reputation and indeed may attack, latching on with a viselike grip that is almost unbreakable; however, like the wolf-eel, morays usually do not strike unless molested.

Leafy Seadragon (*Phycodurus eques*). This odd, foot-long relative of the seahorse looks more like a plant than a fish, and its highly developed camouflage makes it hard to distinguish from the kelp beds where it lives, in the warm coastal waters of Australia. It is a very rare fish, not often sighted; there are currently none in any public aquarium, and only a few dried specimens in museums. It is thought that the female breeds by attaching her eggs to a brood patch on the underside of the male's tail.

Scrawled Cowfish *(Lactophrys quadricornis)*, **Porcupinefish** *(Diodon hystrix)*. These two close cousins look like alien creatures. The scrawled cowfish (top) gets its name from the hornlike projections above its eyes (two others protrude behind). It is a beautiful lemon-yellow with blue markings, but the bony, boxlike armor that encloses its flesh makes it inedible for its would-be predators. The porcupinefish (bottom) is also an unappetizing mouthful. Whenever attacked or disturbed it will swell its body with water or air, which causes its spines to stick out in a defensive array. Despite its grotesque appearance, the porcupinefish is attractively colored, with its brown-spotted back and white belly. When inflated, the spots in back look like huge, glaring eyes.

19

Jewfish *(Epinephelus itajara).* The jewfish, the largest member of the grouper or sea-bass family, has olive-green skin covered with dark spots. Some of these monsters can weigh over 650 pounds. They live in large holes or dens relatively close to shore, and may pounce on passing fish to vary their usual diet of lobsters and other crustaceans. The males seem to turn into females late in life. Although normally sluggish, they can become aggressive; there have been reports of attacks on divers, and some have disappeared in South Pacific areas where jewfish live. But although there is speculation that these fish devour humans, no actual evidence of it has ever been found.

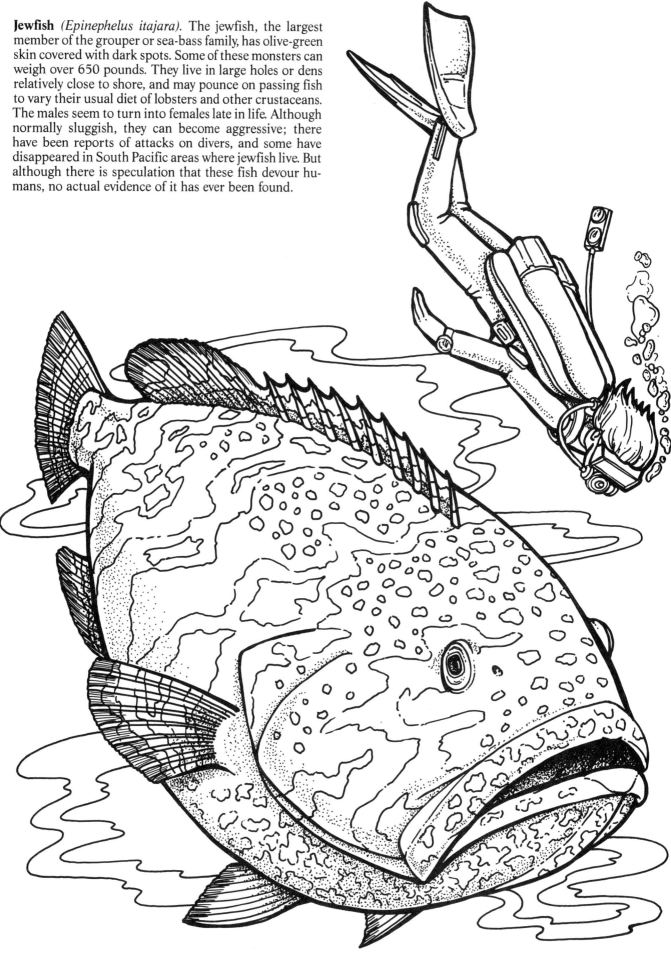

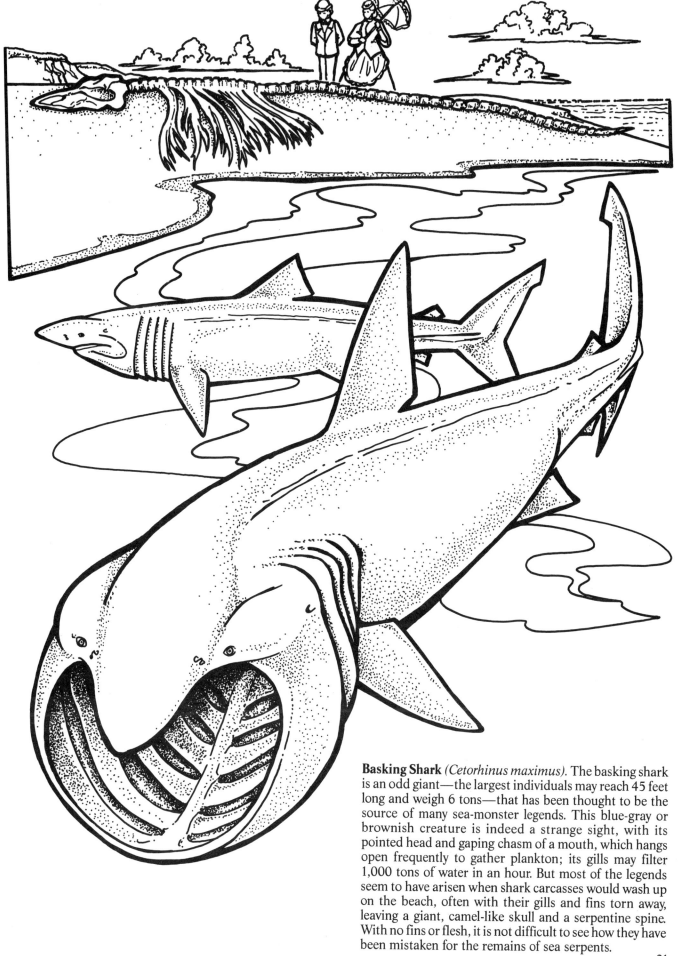

Basking Shark (*Cetorhinus maximus*). The basking shark is an odd giant—the largest individuals may reach 45 feet long and weigh 6 tons—that has been thought to be the source of many sea-monster legends. This blue-gray or brownish creature is indeed a strange sight, with its pointed head and gaping chasm of a mouth, which hangs open frequently to gather plankton; its gills may filter 1,000 tons of water in an hour. But most of the legends seem to have arisen when shark carcasses would wash up on the beach, often with their gills and fins torn away, leaving a giant, camel-like skull and a serpentine spine. With no fins or flesh, it is not difficult to see how they have been mistaken for the remains of sea serpents.

21

Goosefish *(Lophius americanus).* With its yawning, tooth-filled mouth, the goosefish is a monstrous sight indeed. It buries its flat, mottled-brown body in the sand and lures fish to its mouth by waving a fleshy growth attached to its first dorsal spine. When a victim gets close, the goosefish opens its mouth swiftly, creating a vacuum that literally sucks the meal in. Goosefish are indiscriminate feeders that have been known to eat fish as large as themselves—up to 4 feet long—and even diving birds. These giant anglers are found on the Atlantic coast from the Gulf of St. Lawrence down to Argentina.

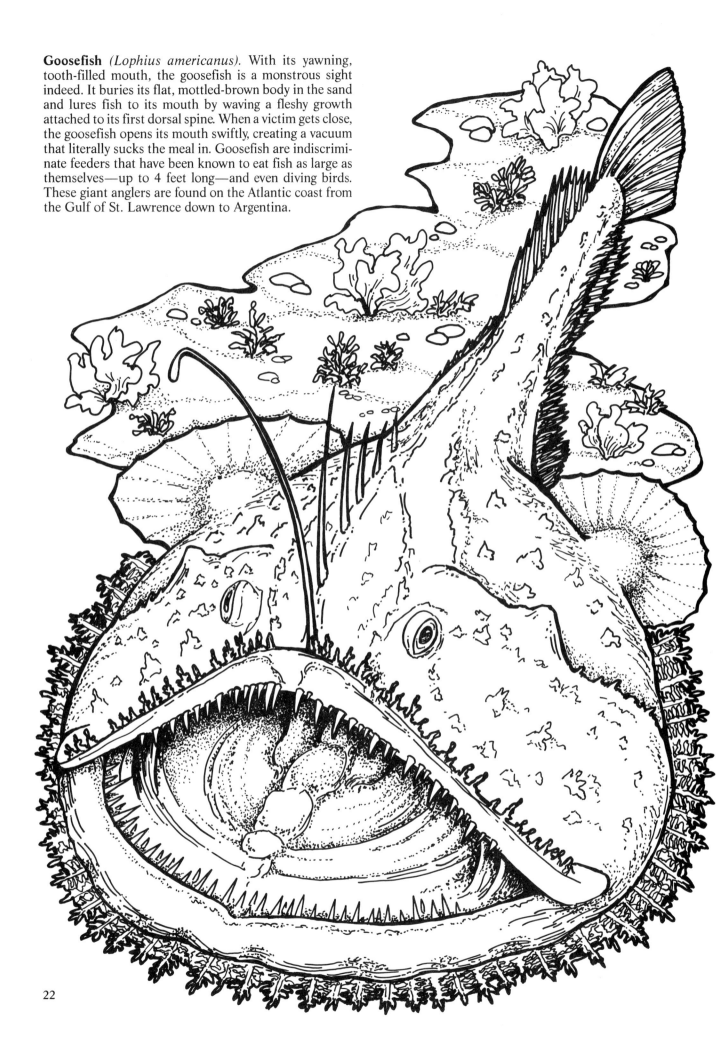

Northern Sea Robin *(Prionotus carolinus)*. The sea robin looks as though it was put together from the parts of several different animals—the body of a fish, the head of a goat, the wings of a bird and humanlike fingers. These fingers are the first three rays of the pectoral fins; thus modified, they help the fish walk over the sandy bottom and locate its normal food of bottom-dwelling crustaceans. It is olive, gray and brown above and pale below, and it may reach a length of over a foot. It is found abundantly in temperate and tropical waters along the Atlantic coast.

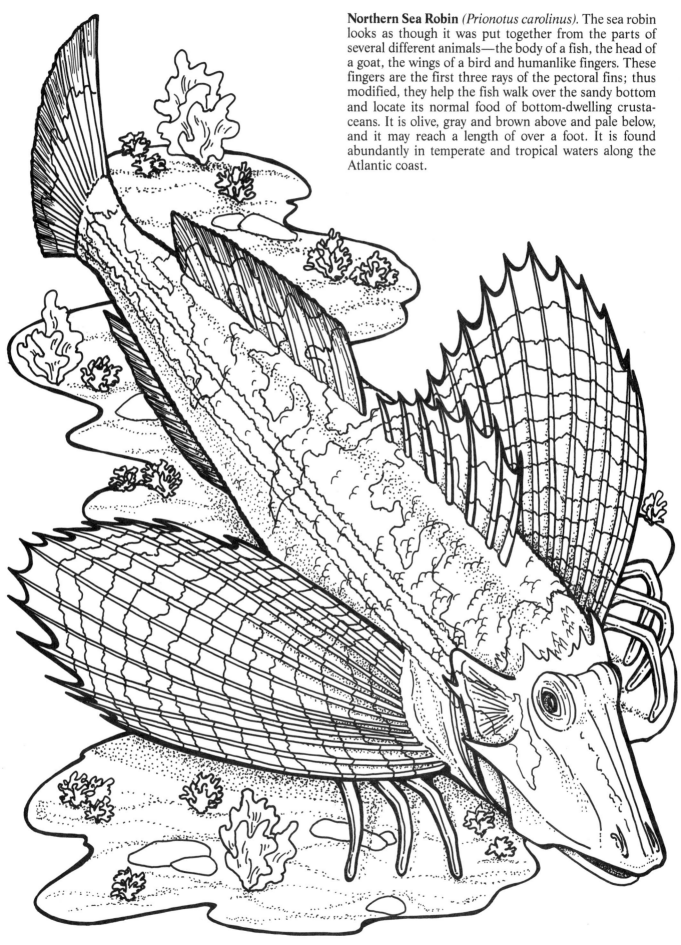

23

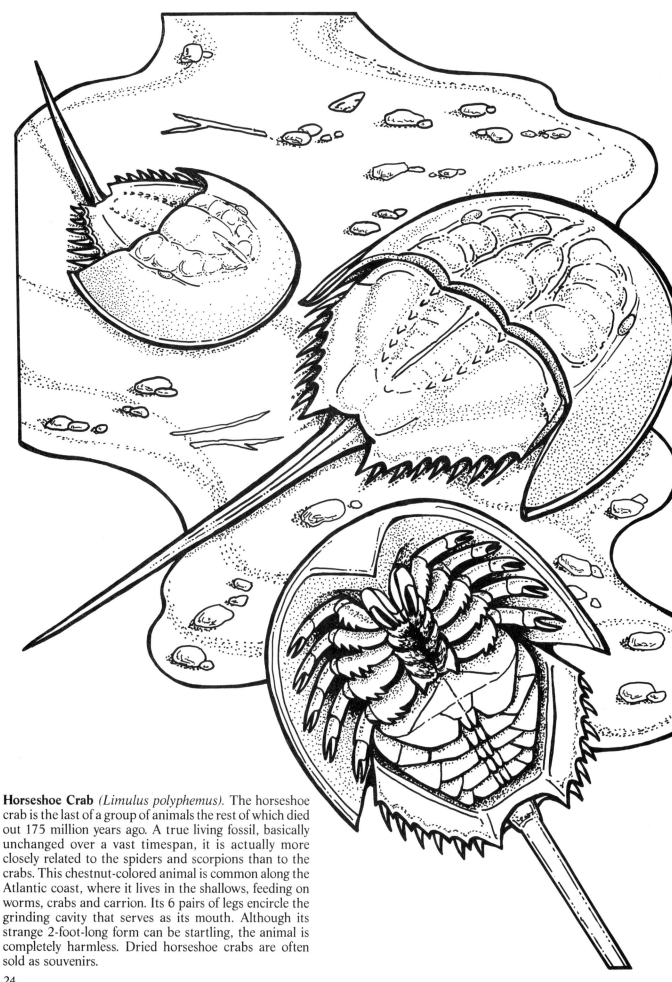

Horseshoe Crab *(Limulus polyphemus).* The horseshoe crab is the last of a group of animals the rest of which died out 175 million years ago. A true living fossil, basically unchanged over a vast timespan, it is actually more closely related to the spiders and scorpions than to the crabs. This chestnut-colored animal is common along the Atlantic coast, where it lives in the shallows, feeding on worms, crabs and carrion. Its 6 pairs of legs encircle the grinding cavity that serves as its mouth. Although its strange 2-foot-long form can be startling, the animal is completely harmless. Dried horseshoe crabs are often sold as souvenirs.

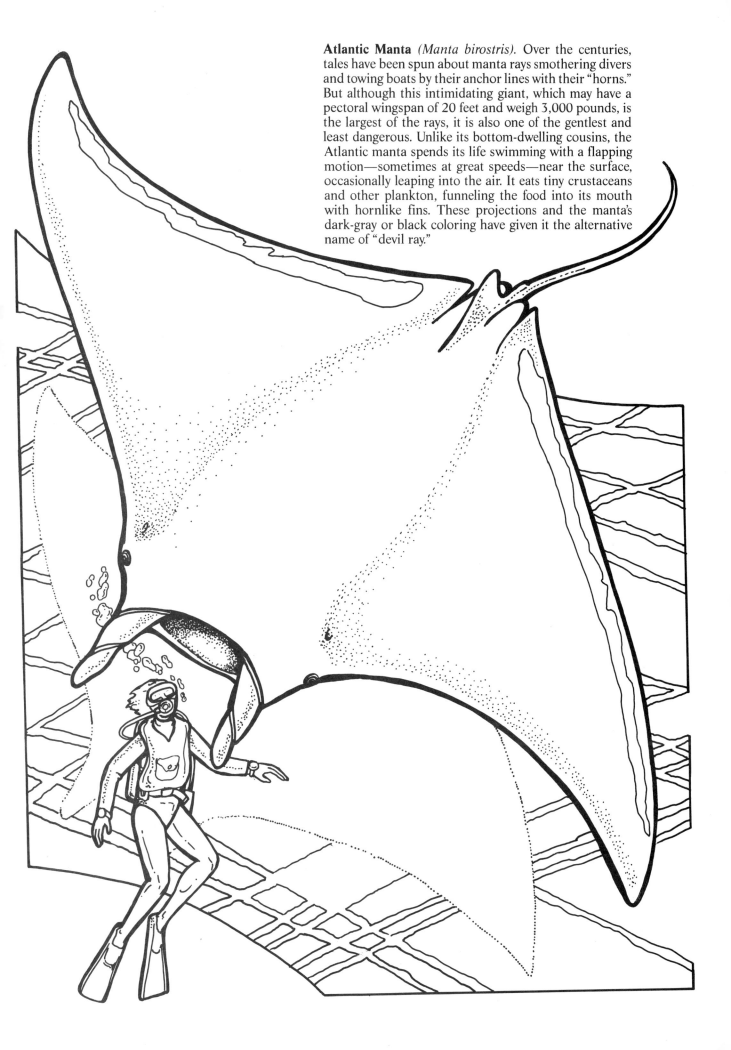

Atlantic Manta *(Manta birostris).* Over the centuries, tales have been spun about manta rays smothering divers and towing boats by their anchor lines with their "horns." But although this intimidating giant, which may have a pectoral wingspan of 20 feet and weigh 3,000 pounds, is the largest of the rays, it is also one of the gentlest and least dangerous. Unlike its bottom-dwelling cousins, the Atlantic manta spends its life swimming with a flapping motion—sometimes at great speeds—near the surface, occasionally leaping into the air. It eats tiny crustaceans and other plankton, funneling the food into its mouth with hornlike fins. These projections and the manta's dark-gray or black coloring have given it the alternative name of "devil ray."

Spotted Ratfish *(Hydrolagus colliei),* **Long-nosed Chi maera** *(Harriotta raleighana).* With cartilage rather than bone for its skeletons, the family of the ratfish and chi maeras is considered a transitional stage between the sharks and the bony fishes. The spotted ratfish (top) gets its name from its rodentlike face and tail. It is usually silver with blue-white spots, and it lives off the Pacific coast from California to Alaska. The long-nosed chi maera (bottom) is an abyssal dweller that lives off the Atlantic coast 2,000–8,000 feet down, and tends to be dark ruddy brown. Both species eat small fish and invertebrates and may grow to a length of 3–4 feet.

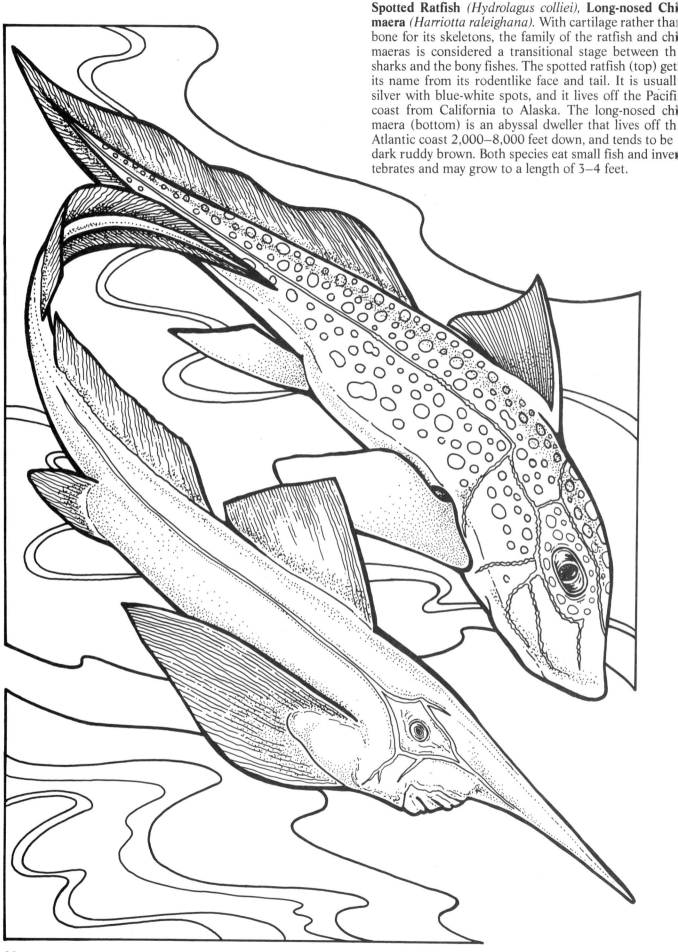

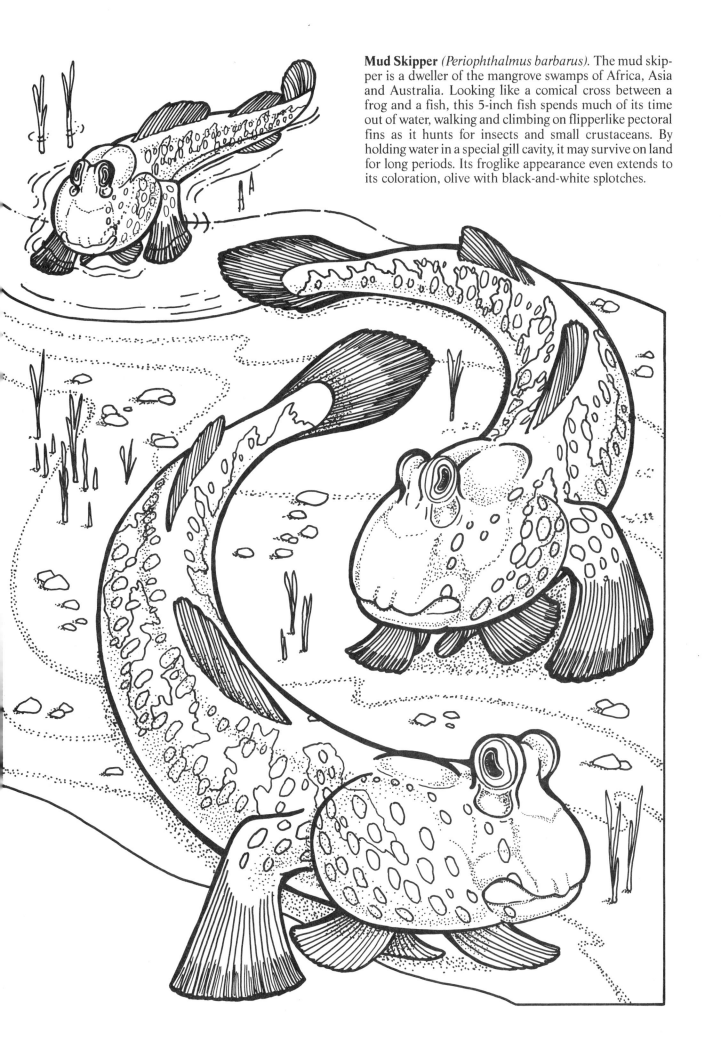

Mud Skipper *(Periophthalmus barbarus)*. The mud skipper is a dweller of the mangrove swamps of Africa, Asia and Australia. Looking like a comical cross between a frog and a fish, this 5-inch fish spends much of its time out of water, walking and climbing on flipperlike pectoral fins as it hunts for insects and small crustaceans. By holding water in a special gill cavity, it may survive on land for long periods. Its froglike appearance even extends to its coloration, olive with black-and-white splotches.

Trumpetfish *(Aulostomus maculatus).* The trumpetfish gets its name from its long hornlike mouth. Living among the coral reefs of the Caribbean, this 2-foot-long fish has the unusual habit of suspending itself with its tail pointing toward the surface and its head toward the bottom. With its mottled-brown-and-white striping, it will float like this, camouflaged among the coral and the water plants, waiting for a fish or shrimp to swim by below. When one comes into its range, it will suck the victim up like a vacuum cleaner.

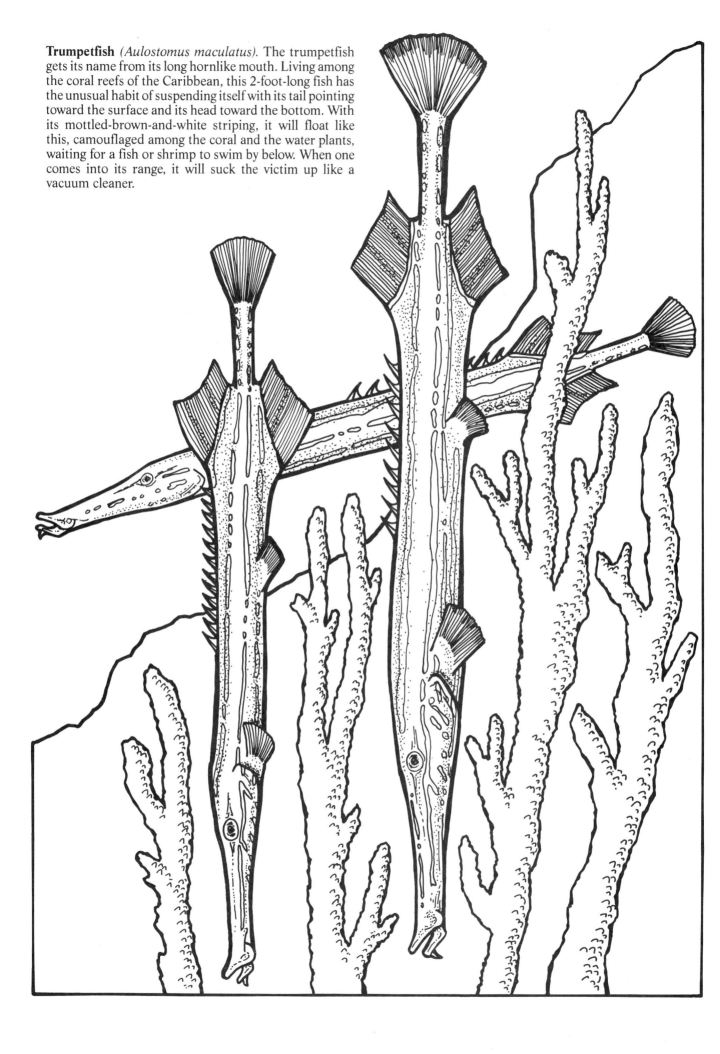

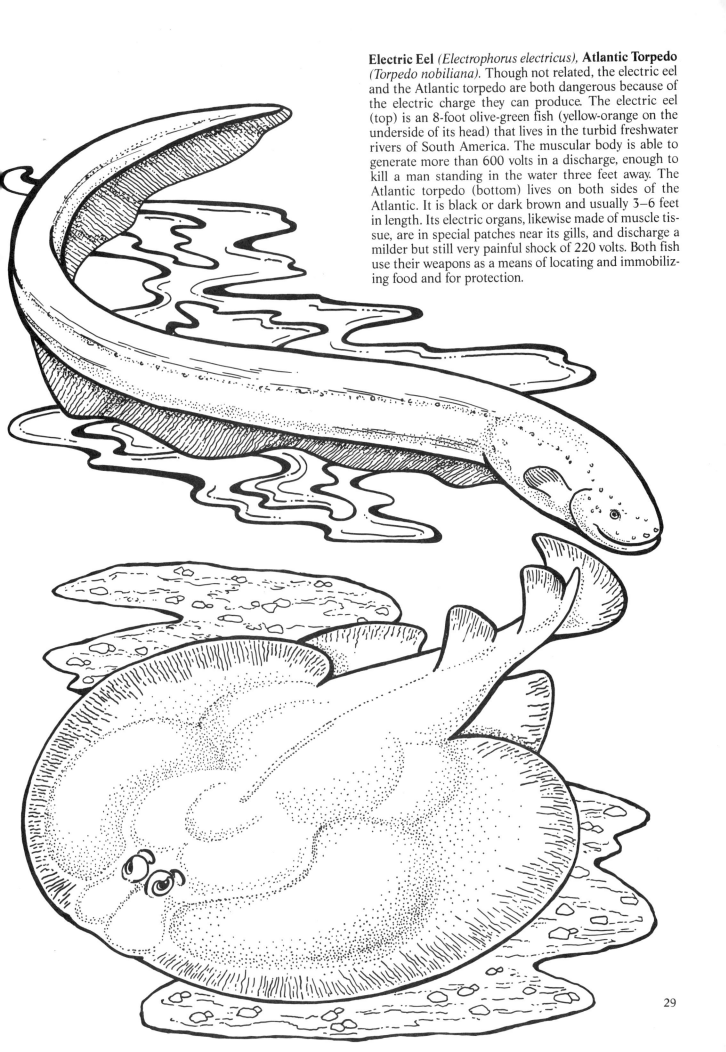

Electric Eel (*Electrophorus electricus*), **Atlantic Torpedo** (*Torpedo nobiliana*). Though not related, the electric eel and the Atlantic torpedo are both dangerous because of the electric charge they can produce. The electric eel (top) is an 8-foot olive-green fish (yellow-orange on the underside of its head) that lives in the turbid freshwater rivers of South America. The muscular body is able to generate more than 600 volts in a discharge, enough to kill a man standing in the water three feet away. The Atlantic torpedo (bottom) lives on both sides of the Atlantic. It is black or dark brown and usually 3–6 feet in length. Its electric organs, likewise made of muscle tissue, are in special patches near its gills, and discharge a milder but still very painful shock of 220 volts. Both fish use their weapons as a means of locating and immobilizing food and for protection.

29

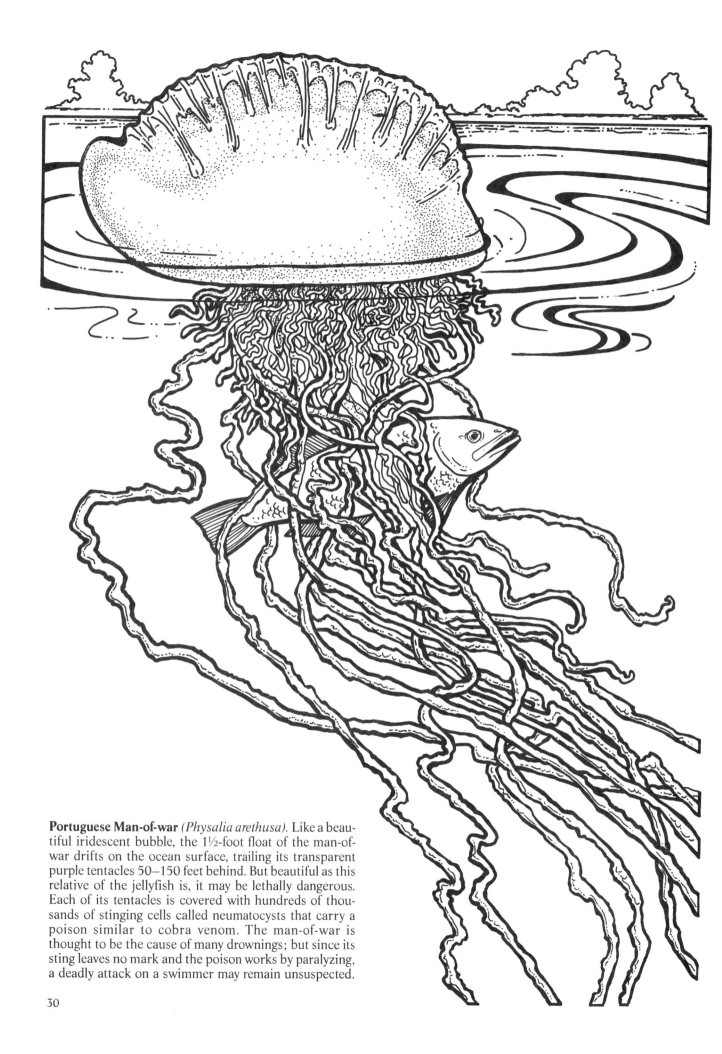

Portuguese Man-of-war *(Physalia arethusa).* Like a beautiful iridescent bubble, the 1½-foot float of the man-of-war drifts on the ocean surface, trailing its transparent purple tentacles 50–150 feet behind. But beautiful as this relative of the jellyfish is, it may be lethally dangerous. Each of its tentacles is covered with hundreds of thousands of stinging cells called neumatocysts that carry a poison similar to cobra venom. The man-of-war is thought to be the cause of many drownings; but since its sting leaves no mark and the poison works by paralyzing, a deadly attack on a swimmer may remain unsuspected.

Giant Clam *(Tridacna gigas).* This 4-foot, 600-pound bivalve of the Indo-Pacific—the legendary man-eating monster—is probably one of the most unjustly maligned of the ocean's creatures. Adventure stories, movies and cartoons have often shown a diver getting his foot caught between the clam's halves, unable to escape. But in truth this is highly unlikely. The clam is usually easy to spot, so few divers would step into it. And the halves close so slowly that divers would have no trouble removing their feet before the shell sealed tightly.

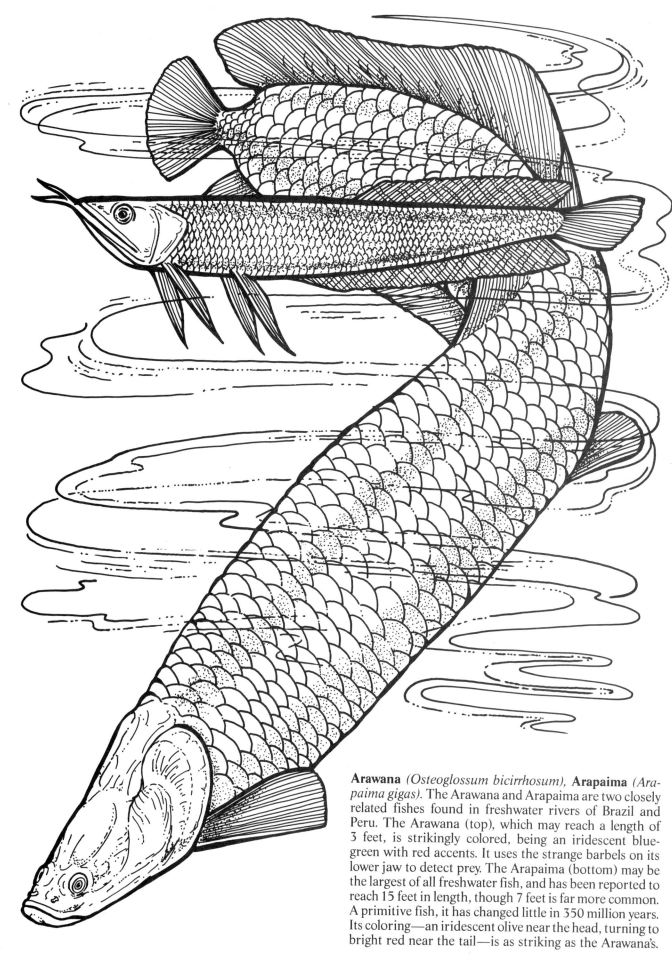

Arawana *(Osteoglossum bicirrhosum)*, **Arapaima** *(Arapaima gigas)*. The Arawana and Arapaima are two closely related fishes found in freshwater rivers of Brazil and Peru. The Arawana (top), which may reach a length of 3 feet, is strikingly colored, being an iridescent blue-green with red accents. It uses the strange barbels on its lower jaw to detect prey. The Arapaima (bottom) may be the largest of all freshwater fish, and has been reported to reach 15 feet in length, though 7 feet is far more common. A primitive fish, it has changed little in 350 million years. Its coloring—an iridescent olive near the head, turning to bright red near the tail—is as striking as the Arawana's.